KS2

D1152375

VISUAL REVISION GUIDE

SUCCESS

Science

Author

Lynn Huggins-Cooper

CONTENTS

PLANTS

ANIMALS AND ECOSYSTEMS

HUMANS

2

MATERIALS

PHYSICAL PROCESSES

TEST, ANSWERS AND GLOSSARY

FLOWER POWER

PARTS OF A FLOWER

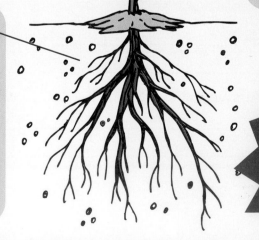

PETAL
The petal is often brightly coloured and scented to attract pollinating *insects.*

LEAF
The leaf acts as a 'food factory' using the energy from sunlight.

ROOT
The root carries water *and* nutrients *from the* soil *to the plant and keeps it* anchored in the ground.

★ **top tip** ★
You can see the internal parts of a flower really clearly in big flowers such as lilies. Have a look!

WHAT'S INSIDE A FLOWER?

The <u>anthers</u>, at the top of the <u>stamens</u> (male), hold the pollen.

The pollen enters the female part of the flower through the <u>stigma</u>.

The <u>ovary</u> contains the <u>ovules</u> (female) that will become seeds.

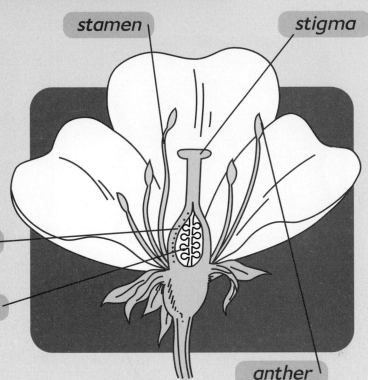

stamen

stigma

ovary

ovules

anther

Did you know that we ate flower buds, roots and stems in that stir-fry at dinnertime?

That's funny – I thought we had broccoli, carrots and celery ...

QUICK TEST

Choose the best word to complete the sentences:

1. The root/stem/petal carries water and nutrients from the soil to the plant and holds the plant in the soil. *Root*

2. The root/petal/leaf is brightly coloured to attract pollinating insects. *petal*

3. The plant makes its food using the energy from the sun. The food is made in the leaf/stem/root . *leaf*

HAVE A GO ...

Tell someone about the parts of a flower and what they do. Use a real plant to help you explain.

ANSWERS 1. Root 2. Petal 3. Leaf

5

TRANSFER OF ENERGY

Grown without sufficient light and water:
Yellowed leaves, spindly growth and shrivelling leaves.

Grown with sufficient light and water:
Green leaves, strong growth and plump, juicy leaves.

GROW, GROW, GROW!

PHOTOSYNTHESIS

Most plants need light and water to grow. Plants use the light energy from the sun to make food in their leaves. This process is called photosynthesis. 'Synthesis' as part of a word usually means 'make', and 'photo' usually means that light is involved. So the word photosynthesis means 'made using light'.

GROWING IN THE DARK

What happens to plants grown in the dark?

If you put plants in the dark, they turn yellow and grow slowly. They need the light energy from the sun to make their food. There is a special green chemical in their leaves called <u>chlorophyll</u> that helps them to do this.

If you grow a plant on a windowsill, the plant grows towards the light.

★ **top tip** ★

Cut a piece of thick paper in the shape of the first letter of your name. Stick it to the top side of a big leaf with sticky tape. Leave it for a couple of weeks and then remove it. Your letter will show up in yellow on the green leaf!

That's funny – I shut Mel in a dark room and she was rather green when SHE came out ...

QUICK TEST

1. Which of the things in this list do plants need to grow healthily? *water light*

   water   soil   light   fertiliser

2. The process that green plants use to make their food is called: *Photosynthesis*

   photography/phototherapy/photosynthesis

HAVE A GO ...

Tell someone what happens to plants if you leave them in a dark place.

ANSWERS   1. Water, light   2. Photosynthesis

FERTILISATION

The *male cells* in the pollen travel down a *tube* into the <u>ovary</u> of the plant, and join the *female cells* in the <u>ovules</u>. This is called <u>fertilisation</u> and it is how *seeds are produced.*

Some seeds such as blackberry pips and rosehips are *spread by animals and birds* when they eat the fruits.

Some seeds are specially <u>adapted</u> to grip onto *fur and feathers.*

Some seeds *travel by water.*

Some seeds *blow on the wind.*

The seed pods of the Himalayan balsam *explode* to scatter the seeds.

★ **top tip** ★

Grow some sprouting seeds such as mung beans or adzuki beans in a jar on the windowsill. You can buy the seeds from health food stores. Put them in a jar and rinse them every day with clean water. They are lovely in sandwiches!

POLLINATION

Once the plant has grown and *produced flowers*, it may be <u>pollinated</u>. This means that the pollen from another plant of the *same type* has landed on the female parts of the plant. The pollen may be *carried on the wind or by insects.*

GERMINATION

Plants go through many *different stages* in their lives.

A seed needs *moisture, air and the correct temperature* to <u>germinate</u> or start to grow.

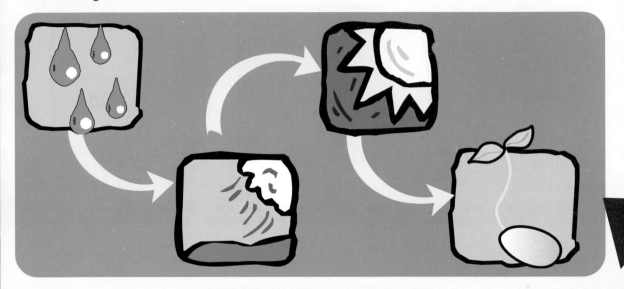

ACORN TO OAK TREE!

QUICK TEST

1. Put these words into the correct order to describe the life cycle of a plant:

   1 pollination 4 germination
   2 fertilisation 3 seed dispersal

2. True or false?

   a. Seeds need moisture to germinate. T
   b. Blackberry seeds are spread by explosions. F
   c. Some seeds are spread by water. T

What stage in life am I at?

An irritating one!

HAVE A GO ...

Can you remember all the ways in which seeds are spread or dispersed?

A HORRIBLE CRIME

A terrible crime has been committed! Two of these plants look a bit *worse for wear*. Have they been looked after properly? Can you find out what went wrong?

PLANT DETECTIVES

WHAT YOU NEED

Three plants.
They must be the same size for this to be a <u>fair test</u>.
Seedlings grown from *sunflower seeds* are a good
choice – not your mum's best geraniums!
Sunflower seeds can be sown in containers on the
windowsill at any time during the year.

Somewhere dark –
a cupboard

Somewhere bright –
a windowsill

A watering can and
water

Three labels – marked 'Plant 1', 'Plant 2' and 'Plant 3'

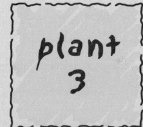

plant
1

plant
2

plant
3

WHAT TO DO

◆ Put a label on each plant pot.
◆ Put plant 1 in a *dark cupboard and keep the soil moist*.
◆ Put plant 2 on a *windowsill and keep it moist*.
◆ Put plant 3 on the same *windowsill, but leave the soil to dry out*.
◆ Write down what you think will happen to the plants.
◆ Leave them where they are for a week, making sure the soil in pot 1
and pot 2 is kept moist.
◆ What happened? Were your predictions correct?

TEST ROUND-UP

SECTION 1

Fill in the missing words from the box below:

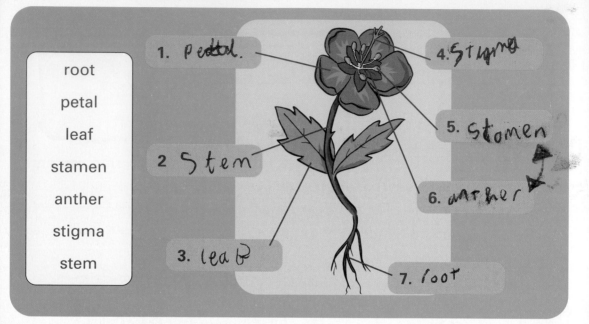

root

petal

leaf

stamen

anther

stigma

stem

1. Pettal.

4. Stigma

2 Stem

5. Stamen

6. anther

3. leaf

7. root

SECTION 2

Join each part of the plant to the correct description with a line.

Plant grown in bright sunlight, plenty of water

Plant grown in the dark, plenty of water

Plant grown in bright sunlight, not enough water

SECTION 3

Put a ring around the correct answers.

1. What does a *seed* need to germinate *or start to grow?*

 moisture  cold  wind  air 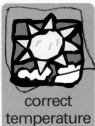 correct temperature  birds

2. Plants may be pollinated by:

 insects  slugs  wind  sunshine

3. Seeds are spread, or dispersed by:

 wind  water  rain  birds  animals

 sunlight  explosions

I never knew wind was so useful!

Me neither! I thought it just pushed clouds along!

★ **top tip** ★

Learn the names of the parts of a plant in the same way as you learn spellings – look, write, cover, check.

CIRCLES OF LIFE

CHANGES ...

All living things change as they grow. Some creatures change more than others.

FROG TIMELINE: A frog starts its life as an egg in a blob of jelly. It emerges as a tadpole and gradually grows into a tiny frog.

frog spawn   tadpole   froglet   frog

LADYBIRD TIMELINE: A ladybird starts life as a tiny yellow egg. When it hatches, it looks like a piece of black tyre rubber covered in bumps. Eventually it settles down in a cocoon to change into an adult ladybird.

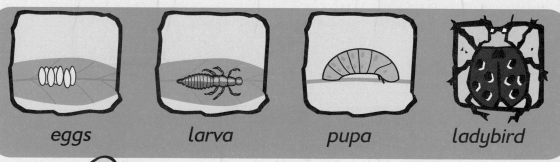

eggs   larva   pupa   ladybird

It's a shame boys don't go through metamorphosis. Sam could do with undergoing a 'great change'!

★ **top tip** ★

Remember the word metamorphosis by thinking about something in a film or videogame that changes before your eyes into something completely different – by MORPHING. 'Meta' means 'great', so metamorphosis means great change.

... MORE CHANGES ...

CHICKEN TIMELINE: A chicken starts life as an egg. It hatches as a downy chick, then grows into a long-legged, skinny pullet. Finally it grows into an adult chicken.

egg   chick   pullet   chicken

HUMAN TIMELINE: A baby is tiny and helpless when it is born. It quickly grows into an inquisitive child, then changes through the process of puberty into an adult.

... AND THE GREAT CHANGE

Some creatures go through a complete change as they grow. The young creature looks nothing like the adult. Animals such as frogs, ladybirds, dragonflies, butterflies, toads and newts come into this group. The change is called <u>metamorphosis</u>.

QUICK TEST

Draw a life cycle timeline like the ones above about a butterfly growing from egg to adult.

HAVE A GO ...

Can you tell someone about the changes that a frog goes through as it grows from egg to adult?

GROOVY GROUPS

CLASSIFICATION KEYS

<u>Classification keys</u> are used to classify or *sort things into groups*. In biology, plants and creatures are classified into different groups according to <u>characteristics</u> that they share. Crabs and lobsters share the characteristic that they *both have shells*, for example.

Classification keys *ask a series of simple questions* to help you to sort things into groups. The questions are usually about some characteristic that a plant or creature has or does not have.

A group of things to be classified:

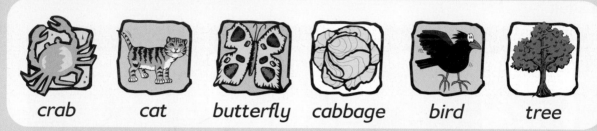

crab   cat   butterfly   cabbage   bird   tree

An example of classification keys:

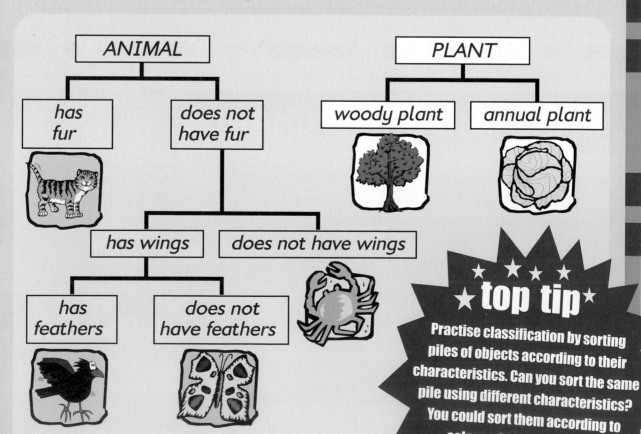

★ **top tip** ★

Practise classification by sorting piles of objects according to their characteristics. Can you sort the same pile using different characteristics? You could sort them according to colour, what they are used for – anything you can think of!

16

VENN DIAGRAMS

<u>Venn diagrams</u> are another way of *sorting things into groups*. They are used in maths as well as science.

When creatures or plants could be members of both sets, they are placed in the *middle part where the circles are joined*. Alligators, turtles and frogs live mostly in water, and also lay eggs, so they are members of both sets.

Perhaps I could use classification to help me sort out all of my CDs ...!

HAVE A GO ...

Cut two paper circles and then cut pictures from magazines or comics to show someone how a Venn diagram works. Choose two characteristics to classify or sort your pictures into groups and show at least one example that is a member of both sets.

QUICK TEST

Make up a classification key to sort out the following creatures and plants:

duck   cow   hen   pig

daisy   turnip   fern   oak tree

ANSWER See page 16 for help.

17

NATURE'S SUPERMARKET

FOOD CHAINS

A <u>food chain</u> tells us about the transfer of energy. It is the simplest way of showing how <u>energy</u> is transferred from <u>organism</u> to organism.

All energy comes originally from the sun. Plants use sunlight to make their own food through a process called <u>photosynthesis</u>.

In a food chain, a plant is called a <u>primary producer</u>, because it *produces food for other creatures.* Remember this by thinking that it is a producer, because it makes or produces food. Primary means it comes first, like *primary school*.

An animal that eats plants is called a <u>herbivore</u>. In a food chain, a herbivore is a <u>primary consumer</u>.

Animals that eat other animals are called <u>carnivores</u>. In a food chain, <u>predators</u> are called <u>secondary</u> or even <u>tertiary consumers</u>, because they come second or third. They are called predators, because they kill other animals and eat them.

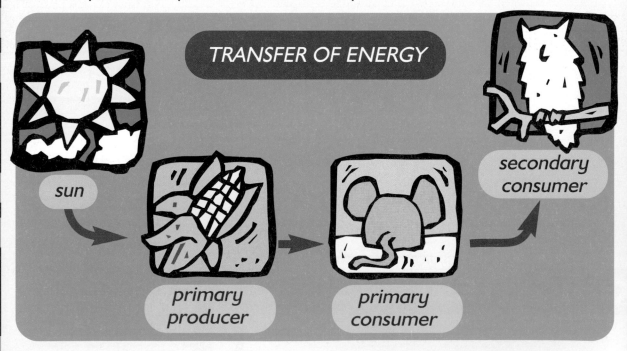

TRANSFER OF ENERGY

sun

primary producer

primary consumer

secondary consumer

In the food chain *sun – corn – fieldmouse – owl*, the corn is the primary producer, the mouse is the primary consumer, and the owl is the secondary consumer.

FOOD WEBS

A <u>food web</u> is more complicated. It involves *connected food chains.*

In a food web made up from *dandelion, rabbit, fox, snail, thrush,* the fox may eat the rabbit, but also may eat the thrush and even the snail. The web looks like this:

★ **top tip** ★

Remember, secondary comes after primary, in the same way as secondary school follows primary school. Tertiary just means third.

If I eat a Giganto Megaburger, does that make me a secondary consumer?

Well, yes... the cow ate grass and the burger is made of beef... but it also makes you a greedy wotsit if you eat all that!

QUICK TEST

1. Put these in order to show a seaside food chain:

   seaweed   sun   shark   crab   bass

2. Match the labels to the plants and animals in this food chain:

1. primary producer	a. hedgehog
2. secondary consumer	b. sun
3. primary consumer	c. slug
4. energy source	d. lettuce

ANSWERS : **1.** Sun, seaweed, crab, bass, shark.
2. 1 = d 2 = a 3 = c 4 = b

HAVE A GO ...

Tell a friend why the sun is so important when we are talking about food chains.

ADAPTABLE ANIMALS

ANIMALS IN THEIR ENVIRONMENT

Wherever animals live they have to adapt to their environment.

Animals who live in the desert, where it is very hot and dry, and animals who live in the Arctic, where it is very cold and bleak, are very well adapted to their harsh environments. If they were not, they would be unable to survive.

Penguins are adapted to the cold by having a thick layer of fat to keep them warm. They also have fine, downy feathers underneath their sleek waterproof feathers. The fluffy layer acts like an insulating duvet and the waterproof outer layer of oily feathers acts like a waterproof jacket. The penguins sometimes seem clumsy on land, but their streamlined shape makes them acrobatic and graceful swimmers.

Camels are adapted to life in the hot, dry desert in many ways. They can go without drinking for long periods by storing water in their specially adapted humps. They also have leathery eyelids and long, silky eyelashes to help protect their eyes from the glare of the sun and the stinging sand. Their feet are flat and splayed, giving them a large surface area. These act like snowshoes, helping the camel to walk without sinking into the sand.

THE PEPPERED MOTH STORY

Animals <u>adapt</u> to their <u>environment</u>. This means that they *change over time* to make themselves fit in with the *conditions* in the place where they live.

The Peppered Moth is a good example. These common moths live in towns and in the country. In the country, they are a creamy white colour with speckles on their wings. In the city, Peppered Moths have much darker grey wings. This colouring has developed to help <u>camouflage</u> them, to keep them safe from <u>predators</u> such as birds. The darker wings blend in with the grime found on many city surfaces where the moths settle.

I wonder if my maths teacher is adapted to life in freezing conditions? He's VERY hairy!

QUICK TEST

Read the description of the planet Plaaarp, and design an alien adapted to the environment.

My planet is Plaaarp! It has three glittering purple suns that shine all the time, so it is very hot. The ground is soft and slushy with the delightful texture of rotting peaches. Water drops from the sky constantly.

★ top tip ★

Look at your pet or an animal you see on the television. How is it adapted to its natural environment or way of life?

HAVE A GO ...

Can you describe how a polar bear is adapted to life in freezing conditions?

THE SEVEN PROCESSES OF LIFE

There are seven life processes that all living things share.

- NUTRITION – they all feed

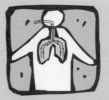

- RESPIRATION – they all breathe

- LOCOMOTION – they all move

- EXCRETION – they all get rid of waste

- SENSITIVITY – they all feel things

- MATURATION – they all grow and change

- REPRODUCTION – they all produce young

I do all those things – I must be alive!

I don't know about the SENSITIVITY part ...

IT'S ALIVE!

IS IT ALIVE?

Deciding if things are alive can be difficult.

It could be hard to decide whether plants were alive if you didn't already know. You can't usually see a plant move (not counting swaying in the wind). Plants do move though, to follow the light. If you grow seedlings on a windowsill, they will bend towards the light. So plants are alive.

Cats are alive – we know that from common sense. However, if we had to explain to an alien, for example, why a cat is alive, we could say the cat:

- eats
- moves
- feels things
- breathes
- gets rid of waste
- grows and changes
- produces young – kittens!

★ top tip ★

Use a mnemonic:* write a silly sentence to help you remember the key words: feeding (f), moving (m), feeling (f), breathing (b), waste (w), growing (g), babies (b). For example, 'friends might fight, but we get better' (f m f b w g b).

* see glossary

QUICK TEST

Which of the things in this list are alive?

How do you know?

1. Stone	2. Cat
3. Stream	4. Cactus
5. Spider	6. Star

ANSWERS 2. Cat, 4. Cactus, 5. Spider

HAVE A GO ...

See if you can remember all seven things that show something is alive.

MINUTE MICROORGANISMS

WHAT IS A MICROORGANISM?

A <u>microorganism</u> is a *very tiny, living thing*. You can work out that it has to be really small from the prefix 'micro'– because you'll need a microscope to see it. Microorganisms include things such as <u>bacteria</u>, <u>viruses</u> and <u>fungi</u>.

Microorganisms can be *harmful* to people.

VIRUSES

Viruses, commonly called germs, make people ill.

Measles
'Flu
Mumps

These illnesses are all caused by micro-organisms called viruses.

BACTERIA

Bacteria can also make people ill. Bacteria can cause stomach upsets and even food poisoning. That is why *food hygiene is so important*.

Salmonella
Gastroenteritis
Ear infections

These illnesses are all caused by micro-organisms called bacteria.

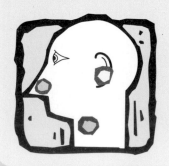

FUNGI

Some fungi, such as the green mould that attacks bread, is also harmful, because it causes food to spoil and can make people ill if they eat it.

HELPFUL MICROORGANISMS

Yeast is used to make beer and bread. <u>Bacteria</u> is also used in the production of yoghurt.

beer

bread

yoghurt

The <u>microorganisms</u> that help rot down compost, are also helpful, because they *break down waste* such as fallen leaves and dead animals.

compost

★ **top tip** ★

Remember, a microorganism is very small, so you cannot see it without a microscope. Even if your hands look clean, they can still be teeming with microorganisms – so always wash them before you eat!

Yes... so why does Mum make us wash our hands?

So bacteria can be really useful?

QUICK TEST

1. How can microorganisms be helpful to people?

2. Name three harmful effects of microorganisms.

3. Name three types of microorganisms.

ANSWERS 1. By breaking down waste. **2.** Causing stomach upsets, spreading germs, making food mouldy. **3.** Viruses, bacteria, fungi.

HAVE A GO ...

Design a poster to encourage people to remember hygiene when they are preparing food.

25

WHAT IS A HABITAT?

A <u>habitat</u> is a word used to describe the place where a *collection of plants and animals* live. Habitats include such places as the *seashore, forest, garden, wasteland, jungle* and *desert*.

A <u>community</u> is the name given to the animals and plants that live together in a *particular place*.

An <u>ecosystem</u> is the scientific term that describes the *community and its habitat*.

<u>Ecology</u> is the study of the *relationship between animals, plants and their surroundings*.

★ **top tip** ★

What sorts of habitats are there near where you live? See if you can classify them – urban, meadow, seashore, etc.

THE GREAT WEB OF LIFE

Creatures and plants living within a particular habitat, such as a tropical rainforest, are all *linked in a great web of life*. They also *compete with each other for food,* and only the strongest, best-adapted creatures *survive and breed*.

In the tropical rainforest, <u>food chains</u> and <u>webs</u> help to maintain the *balance of nature*. Increases in the size of populations are limited by the amount of food available.

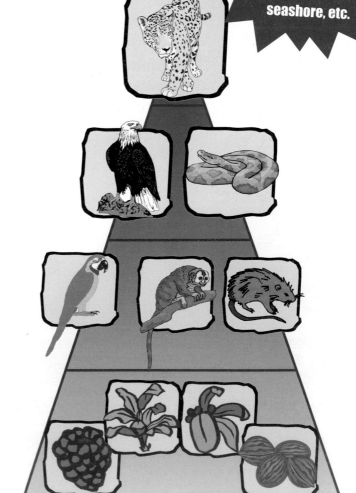

THERE'S NO PLACE LIKE HOME!

LIFE IN A COMMUNITY

There are always more <u>organisms</u> at the bottom of a *food web* than at the top. This is because *the energy passed along is reduced with each link in the food chain.*

All life in a community is linked, so if for some reason one <u>species</u> is wiped out – say a disease killed all the rodents in the forest – *the rest of the community would be affected.* The <u>carnivores</u> would have to *compete more for food* and some could *die through starvation.* The nuts and seeds no longer eaten by the rodents would grow into trees and shrubs, and smaller species of plants could *die through lack of light* as they are covered by the large growth.

I'm off hunting for a fierce, top predator in a dangerous and complex ecosystem!

Oh, going out in the garden looking for the cat, are you?

QUICK TEST

Match the correct word to its definition:

1. habitat

2. ecosystem

3. community

4. ecology

a. Place where a collection of plants and animals live.

b. Animals and plants that live together in a particular place.

c. Scientific term to describe a community and its habitat.

d. The study of the environment.

ANSWERS   1 = a   2 = c   3 = b   4 = d.

HAVE A GO ...

What do you think might happen to the hedgehog population in a garden habitat if all the slugs and snails were killed off by poisoning?

WHAT YOU NEED

What conditions do woodlice prefer? You are going to carry out an experiment to find out.

You need:

◆ Cardboard box, such as a shoebox
◆ Two extra cardboard sheets
◆ Plastic bag
◆ Soil
◆ Transparent food wrap
◆ Woodlice

plastic bag

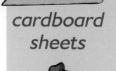
cardboard sheets

soil

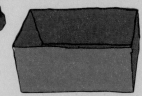
cardboard box

food wrap

WHAT TO DO

◆ Cut a doorway in the centre of the two pieces of extra cardboard sheet.

◆ Stick the extra card down so it makes two rooms in the shoebox, with a corridor in the middle (see diagram opposite).

◆ Line the bottom of each half of the box with a piece of plastic cut from the bag, to stop the cardboard going soggy.

◆ Put dry soil in each side of the box, and dampen one side.

◆ Put several woodlice in the corridor in the centre of the box, then cover the top of the damp end with card so that it is dark, and cover the other end with pierced, transparent food wrap, so it is light.

You could also try to repeat the experiment with four sections in your box – so you had:

◆ damp + dark.
◆ damp + light.
◆ dry + dark.
◆ dry + light.

★ **top tip** ★
Be careful not to harm the woodlice and put them back where you found them as soon as you have finished your experiment.

28

THE AMAZING WOODLOUSE SORTING MACHINE!

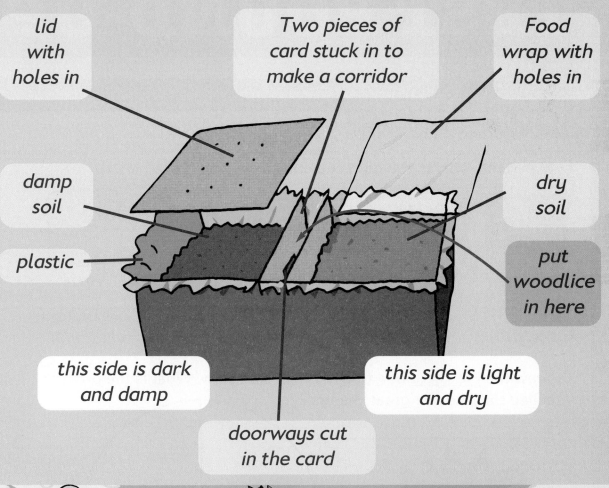

lid with holes in

Two pieces of card stuck in to make a corridor

Food wrap with holes in

damp soil

dry soil

plastic

put woodlice in here

this side is dark and damp

this side is light and dry

doorways cut in the card

HAVE A GO ...

Try to predict where the woodlice will go – and give reasons for your predictions!

SECTION 1

What is a:

1. Habitat _____

2. Community _____

3. Ecosystem _____

TEST ROUND-UP

SECTION 2

1. Match the label to the correct picture in this food chain:

seaweed   *periwinkle*   *crab*   *otter*

| *secondary consumer* | *top carnivore* | *primary consumer* | *primary producer* |

2. Draw the <u>life cycle</u> of a frog in the circle below. What is the process called that means 'great change'?

_____

top tip

Some of this work is quite complicated – when you have learned the facts, get a friend to test you.

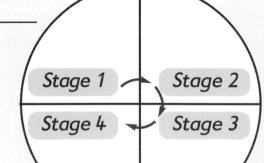

Stage 1 → Stage 2

Stage 4 ← Stage 3

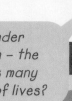

30

Did you know that Alexander Fleming discovered penicillin – the antibiotic mould that cures many diseases and saves millions of lives?

SECTION 3

How is a beaver adapted to life in and around a river?
Tick the correct boxes.

☐ Thick, waterproof fur   ☐ Fine, thin silky fur
☐ Wide tail like a paddle   ☐ Thin tail
☐ Tiny, sharp teeth for fighting   ☐ Large front teeth for gnawing

SECTION 4

Use the Venn diagram below to sort these animals into groups:

has shell   has claws

crab   lobster   parrot   clam   cat

SECTION 5

Match the microorganism to the correct result:

*That's an easy
discovery – just look
in the old pizza boxes
under my bed!*

fungus   mouldy bread

bacteria   'flu

virus   gastroenteritis

THE CIRCULATORY SYSTEM

Have you noticed that when you cut yourself, blood wells up out of the cut, even after you have wiped it away? Have you ever wondered why it keeps appearing? The <u>circulatory system</u>, the name given to *the system that moves blood around your body*, is driven by a *very strong pump* – your heart. Sometimes, people have the idea that your body is filled up with blood in the same way as a vase is filled up with water, but that is not true. Your blood is *constantly moving*, carrying *food and oxygen* to all the cells in your body.

The heart is a powerful pump.

It does not look like the hearts you see on Valentine cards.

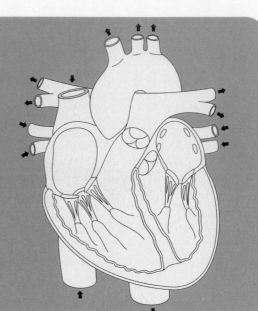

PUMP IT UP!

HOW IT WORKS

Inside, the heart is divided into four hollow 'chambers' or compartments. There are two on the left and two on the right. The upper chambers receive blood returning to the heart through the veins. The lower chambers force blood out of the heart into the arteries to be carried through the body.

Arteries cary blood pumped powerfully at high pressure. That is why it is so dangerous to cut an artery. Because the blood is under so much pressure, it spurts out of any cuts in arteries.

WHAT IS BLOOD MADE UP OF?

We think of blood as a red liquid, but if you looked at blood under a strong microscope you would see several different things:

Red cells

These look like red saucers. They carry the dissolved oxygen around the body.

White cells

These attack invading microbes and fight disease.

Platelets

These are bits of dead cells. They clump together and help to clot your blood. When you cut yourself, platelets seal the hole to make a scab.

Plasma

This is the liquid that contains proteins, salts and sugars.

★ **top tip** ★

It's easy to remember that arteries carry blood away from the heart, because 'art' is at the beginning of the word 'artery'.

he—art—ery

No, but I did know that maths tests make my heart beat faster ...

Did you know that when you do exercise, like in PE, your heart beats faster and your pulse rate goes up?

QUICK TEST

Finish these sentences:

1. Blood is made up of four parts:

2. How many chambers are there inside the heart?

3. Why is it particularly dangerous to cut an artery?

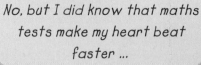

ANSWERS **1.** red cells, white cells, platelets, plasma **2.** 4. **3.** because the blood is under a great deal of pressure and would spurt out of a cut.

HAVE A GO ...

Make up a mnenonic to remind yourself what blood is made up of. For example:
- **rich** (red cells)
- **women** (white cells)
- **please** (platelets)
- **Pluto** (plasma)

SAY CHEESE!

TYPES OF TEETH AND THEIR JOB

Teeth are tools for eating food and in some animals they are also used for defence.

Here are the teeth of three different animals. Look at the different shapes of the teeth.

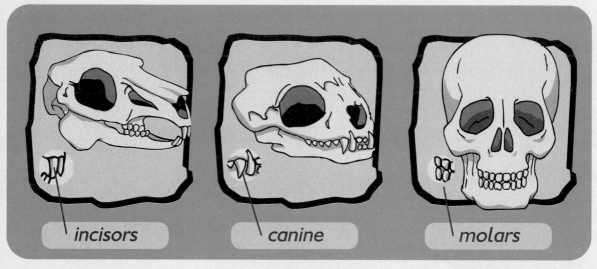

incisors *canine* *molars*

Large <u>incisor</u> teeth for *cutting and cropping* grass.

Sharp <u>canine teeth</u> for *tearing* food such as meat.

Flat <u>molars</u> for *grinding and chewing* food.

<u>Herbivorous</u> animals, such as those that eat grass, like sheep and cows, have flat, wide teeth for *grinding and chewing* tough stems. <u>Carnivorous</u> animals, like cats and dogs, have sharper, pointed teeth for *tearing and chewing* meat and sinews. These animals are often <u>predators</u>.

★ **top tip** ★

Eating cheese at the end of a meal can help to neutralise the acids in your mouth and reduce the chance of tooth decay occurring.

34

CARING FOR YOUR TEETH

You must take *very good care of your teeth*. Cleaning your teeth, using floss and mouthwash, helps to keep your teeth and gums free from the *sticky plaque* that causes *decay*. <u>Plaque</u> is caused by <u>bacteria</u> *acting on the sugars* left on your teeth after you have eaten.

You should also visit the dentist on a regular basis, so that he or she can check that there are no problems.

Would you like an apple?

Fangs a lot!

QUICK TEST

Match the type of tooth to the correct description.

1. canine	2. molars	3. incisor
a. for grinding and chewing food	b. teeth for cutting and cropping grass	c. teeth for tearing food such as meat

4. The Venusian Blargle eats grass and woody plants. Describe what sort of teeth they need.

5. The Venusian Blargle is hunted by a fierce predator, the Snortwoggle. What sort of teeth does a Snortwoggle need?

HAVE A GO ...

Design a leaflet describing how to keep your teeth healthy.

ANSWERS 1 = c 2 = a 3 = b 4. Incisors and molars. 5. Canine.

RATTLE THOSE BONES!

WHY DO YOU HAVE A SKELETON?

Your skeleton has *three jobs*:

1. **Support**
   It stops you from flopping about. Your skeleton acts like *scaffolding* to prop up the *soft tissues* your body is made from.

2. **Protection**
   Your *skull* is a *hard bony case* that protects your *brain*. In the same way, your *ribs* protect your *lungs and heart*, and your *pelvis* protects many of your soft <u>internal organs</u>.

3. **Movement**
   Your *bones are rigid*, but the joints, together with the muscles, help you to *move about*.

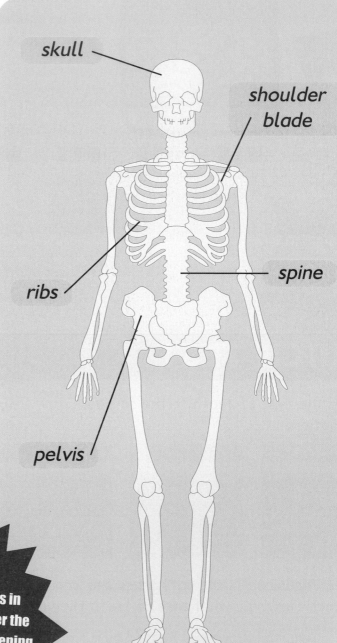

skull

shoulder blade

spine

ribs

pelvis

★ **top tip** ★

Can you tighten the muscles in your body and feel them under the skin? You could have fun tightening and loosening muscles in your face too – as long as no one thinks you're being rude!

JOINTS AND MUSCLES

Have you ever bent your arm up and made a fist to show how big your muscles are? When you do that, you are moving a <u>hinge joint</u> at the elbow and you are showing how *muscles tighten and loosen* to make the arm *work like a lever*.

MUSCLES IN YOUR ARM

To move your arm, different muscles have to work together.

When you bend your arm up to '*show your muscles*', your <u>biceps</u> (bulgy muscle on the top side of your arm) *tighten up* and the smaller <u>triceps</u> on the underside of your arm *relax*. When you straighten your arm again, the *opposite happens*: your biceps relax and your triceps contract.

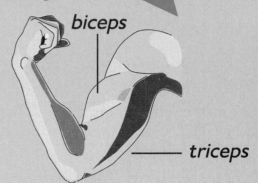

biceps

triceps

So it's because of my skull that it doesn't hurt when I head a football?

No, it's because you don't have a brain ...

QUICK TEST

1. What are the three main functions of bones in our bodies?

2. Name four major bones in the human body.

3. Fill in the missing words:

   The _____ is the bulgy muscle on the top side of your arm. The _____ is the smaller muscle on the underside of your arm.

HAVE A GO ...

Can you explain to someone what is happening when you 'show your muscles'?

ANSWERS 1. Support, protection and movement. 2. Skull, shoulder blade, spine and pelvis. 3. Biceps, triceps.

FULL OF BEANS!

A HEALTHY DIET

We hear lots said about eating a healthy diet, but what does it really mean? There is no such thing as a bad food, but there are foods you should eat regularly.

We need:

<u>Protein</u> – in foods such as milk and cheese.

<u>Carbohydrate</u> – in pasta, bread and cereals.

<u>Fats</u> – in foods such as butter and cooking oil.

<u>Fibre</u> – in vegetables, fruit and cereals.

So no more burgers, then?

Burgers are yummy now and again, but it might be worth ordering strawberries for pudding!

FOOD GROUPS

Protein, carbohydrate, fats and fibre are called food groups. What job does each food group do?

◆ Protein is used by the body for building cells. Protein helps you to grow and repairs damage to the body.

◆ Carbohydrate is the body's main source of fuel. Carbohydrate gives you lots of energy.

◆ Fats are also a source of energy, but this is stored for times when you have no carbohydrate to burn.

◆ Fibre is needed to help you digest your food and keep the whole of your digestive system in good working order.

Remember that no foods are bad, but some, such as those containing high levels of salt and fat, should be eaten in small quantities.

★ **top tip** ★

Did you know that over 75% of your body is made up from water? That's why we need to drink plenty of healthy drinks such as water, juice and milk.

QUICK TEST

Make up a picnic from the items shown in the picture above. Include foods from all the groups, i.e. protein, fats, carbohydrate, fibre.

ANSWER See page 38 for help.

HAVE A GO ...

Look at your lunchbox or your dinner tonight. What food groups are you eating?

KEEPING FIT AND HEALTHY

EXERCISE

A lot of things happen to our bodies when we exercise.

Have you ever been out of breath after you have run about? This happens because your muscles use up lots of oxygen when you exercise. Your body needs oxygen quickly, so you breathe faster and more deeply.

You can also measure the effect of exercise by taking your <u>pulse</u>. When you are resting, your pulse beats at a normal rate. When you exercise, it gets faster. Once you stop, it returns gradually to the normal rate.

PULSE RATE

Here is a graph recording Sam's change of pulse rate.

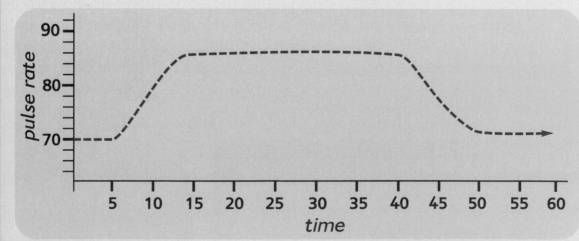

Sam has been playing basketball. See if you can tell from the graph when he started to play. Can you tell when his pulse rate returned to normal?

FIND YOUR OWN PULSE

◆ You can *find your pulse* by pressing down with the first two fingers of your right hand on the inside of your left wrist.

◆ Using a watch or clock with a second hand, *count how many beats you feel in a minute* after resting, and write it down.

◆ Then jump up and down until you feel puffed and count for another minute.

Was there a difference? How long did it take for your pulse to slow back down to its *normal rate*?

◆ Try different activities such as running, cycling and playing sports.

Which activity makes your pulse rate quickest? Why do you think this is?

SECTION 1

1. What are the food groups we need for a healthy diet?

_____

_____

2. Circle the healthier option in each pair:

apple   apple pie   grated   carrot cake
                          carrot

fresh   strawberry   oranges   orange
strawberries   jam   squash

Can you give reasons for your answer?

_____

_____

_____

_____

3. Why do we need fibre in our diets?

_____

_____

_____

_____

4. Draw a healthy dinner with food chosen from the basket below:

TEST ROUND-UP

SECTION 2

1. Why do herbivorous animals, like sheep and cows, have flat, wide teeth?

   _____

2. Why do carnivorous animals, like cats and dogs, have sharper, pointed teeth? _____

3. Circle the correct names of types of teeth:

   incisor   indicator   omnivores   molar   mole

   molecular   canine   ceramic   capillaries

4. What are the three functions of the skeleton?

   _____

5. What are the names of the four things found in blood?

   _____

6. Fill in the missing words:

   Red cells carry _____ around the body.

   White blood cells attack _____ and fight disease.

I'm no good at tests ...

You're good at testing Mum's patience ...

43

MATERIALS MYSTERY!

WHAT ARE MATERIALS?

The word materials describes what items are made from. A door may be made from the material wood, for example, and a window may be made from the material glass. Within your home, you will find items made from many different materials. Take a look and see how many you can identify!

I always thought material just meant the stuff clothes and curtains were made from!

No, Sam – that's FABRIC!

CHOOSING MATERIALS

When objects are designed, the materials they are to be made from is considered carefully. They are chosen according to the characteristics of the materials and the job they will be required to do. To get a picture of how important it is to choose the correct materials, consider the following:

A **window** made from **fabric**.

A **door** made from **paper**.

A **mattress** made from **stone**.

A **chair** made from **glass**.

What would be the problem with choosing these materials in each case? Ask yourself questions about the properties of each material and the job it has to do. Is it:

◆ hard/soft
◆ a heat conductor/not a heat conductor
◆ pliable/brittle
◆ opaque/transparent

★ top tip ★

Always try to think about the properties of each material and how this affects whether it is chosen during the design of an object.

QUICK TEST

1. How many materials can you identify in the picture?

2. Why do you think each particular material was chosen?

HAVE A GO ...

Look around your room – how many different materials can you see? Why do you think they were chosen?

ANSWERS 1. Plastic, metal, cotton, paper, leather, wood, china. 2. See pages 45 and 45 for help.

FILTRATION FUN!

PROBLEM SOLVING

It is useful to think about the <u>properties of materials</u> when you have a problem to solve. Imagine you have a younger sister or brother who wants to play in their paddling pool, but the pool is full of leaves and broken twigs. You could pick out every piece by hand – but it would take you a very long time! Alternatively, you could use a scientific approach and clean out the pool using <u>filtration</u>.

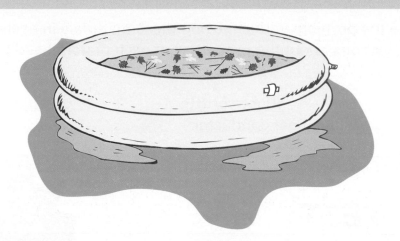

My teacher said I was insoluble!

No, she said INTOLERABLE, silly!

SEPARATION

Filtration is used wherever the solids to be separated from the liquid are <u>insoluble</u> – they will *not dissolve*. Filtration would be used to carry out an experiment at school, if you were asked to separate sand from water.

What equipment would you choose? You know that *sand is insoluble in water*, so you would choose equipment to *filter the mixture*.

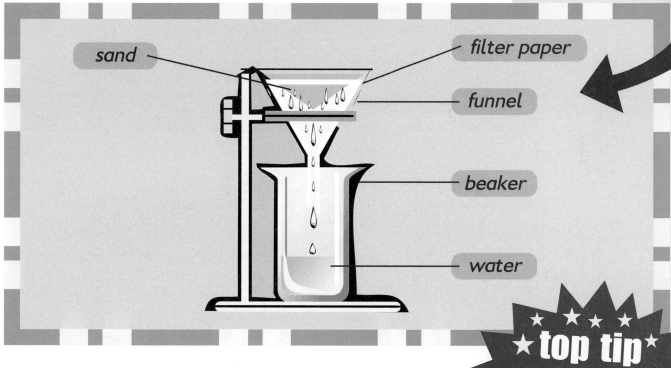

sand
filter paper
funnel
beaker
water

★ **top tip** ★

Look around at home and see if you can see any examples of filtration. If your parents make coffee using ground coffee, there's one for a start!

QUICK TEST

1. What word is used to describe:
   a material that will not dissolve in a particular liquid?

2. What word describes:
   the process of separating a solid that does not dissolve from a liquid?

3. What equipment would you choose to:
   separate grit from water?

HAVE A GO ...

Can you remember what *properties of materials* means? If not, look it up in the glossary at the back of this book!

ANSWERS **1.** Insoluble **2.** Filtration **3.** Funnel, filter paper and beaker.

DISSOLVING

When we say that a material has dissolved, we mean that it is <u>soluble</u> – it will combine with a liquid. Think of gravel in water and sugar in coffee. It does not matter how much we stir or heat the water with gravel, the gravel will not dissolve. However, when we put a spoonful of sugar in a cup of coffee and stir, the sugar gradually combines with the coffee – we can no longer hear it grinding on the side of the cup.

Think also about tasting sea water when you are swimming. You cannot see the salt in the water, as it is dissolved – but you know it is there from the salty taste.

NOW YOU SEE IT, NOW YOU DON'T!

EVAPORATION

On page 46 you read about <u>filtration</u>. <u>Evaporation</u> is another way of separating materials. Unlike filtration, evaporation can separate dissolved solids from liquids. The liquid is heated and as the steam rises (see changing states on page 50), it hits a cold surface and changes back into a liquid. This process is called <u>condensation</u>. The liquid is then collected in a beaker. This carries on until all that is left in the original container is the solid.

★ **top tip** ★

Collect some solids from the kitchen food cupboard (NOT the cleaning cupboard, as some kitchen cleaners are dangerous) and stir them into a cup of water. Do they dissolve? Does it make a difference if you use warm tap water?

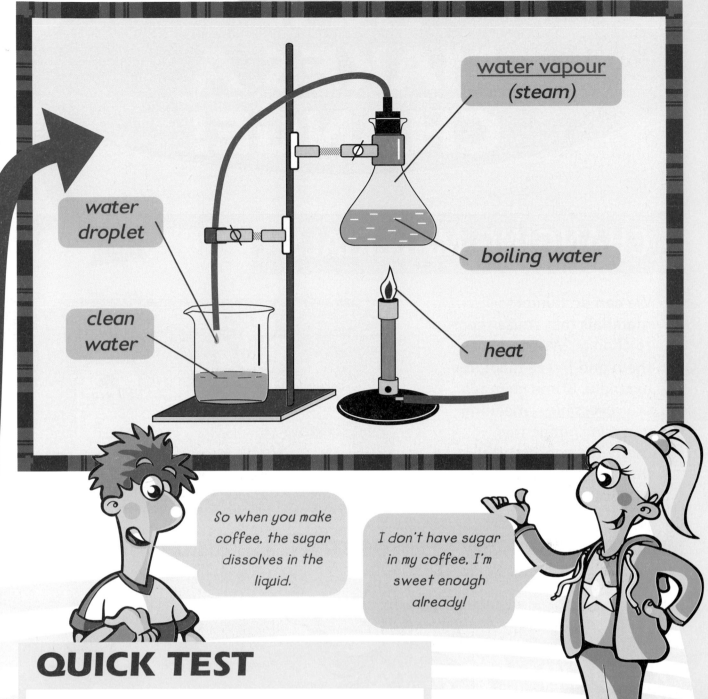

water vapour
(steam)

water droplet

clean water

boiling water

heat

So when you make coffee, the sugar dissolves in the liquid.

I don't have sugar in my coffee, I'm sweet enough already!

QUICK TEST

1. Which of these materials will dissolve in water?

   sand   glitter   salt   bath crystals
   gravel   sugar

2. Using the items below, explain how you would set up an experiment to show how to separate salt from water.

   2 beakers   water
   a stirrer   tripod or stand
   cold surface   nightlight
   salt crystals

HAVE A GO ...

Can you see evidence of condensation anywhere at home?

49

THAT MAKES A CHANGE!

CHANGING MATERIALS

We can do things to materials that *cause them to change*. We can *heat* them and *freeze* them, for example. Some changes are <u>reversible</u> – meaning you can *change the materials back* to what they were in the beginning – but others are not.

★ **top tip** ★

Remember that a reversible change takes a material back to where it started – like reversing a car!

All this talk of food is making me hungry.

Me too – let's go and make some irreversible changes to the fridge!

REVERSIBLE CHANGES

Imagine you are *melting some butter*, ready to make flapjacks. However, if you *took too long* to weigh out the other ingredients, the *butter would go hard again*! Butter melts when it is heated, but when it cools again, it goes hard. This is a <u>reversible change</u>. If you made a chocolate cake, you might melt chocolate to spread on the top of the cake. You have to spread the chocolate quickly, because as it *cools, it will harden*. This is another reversible change.

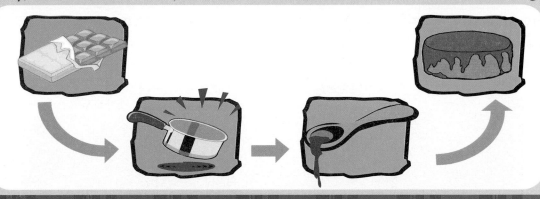

MORE REVERSIBLE CHANGES

Imagine you are making ice lollies from fruit juice. You pour the *juice* into moulds and *put them in the freezer*. When you get them out later, the *lollies are hard*. Imagine you *leave one on the counter* for a while. When you came back, what would you find? A *pool of juice*! Freezing juice or water is another reversible change.

QUICK TEST

Fill in the missing words from the box below:

1. I left some chocolate in my car and it
    _____. I put it in the fridge and it
    went _____ again.

2. So it was a _____ change. When ice
    melts, it turns back into _____. This
    is also a reversible _____.

    hard   melted   water   change   reversible

ANSWERS 1. Melted, hard   2. Reversible, water, change

HAVE A GO ...

Can you explain what happens to each material as it changes? Try putting chocolate in your pocket (keep it in the wrapper), then put it in the fridge. Try leaving butter out on the table in a warm room, then put it in the fridge.

51

ALL CHANGE!

CHANGING MATERIALS

We know that we can do things to materials to cause them to change. We also know that some changes are reversible – and some are not. Irreversible changes are changes that cannot be reversed, like burning wood or frying eggs.

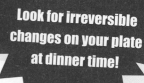

★ top tip ★
Look for irreversible changes on your plate at dinner time!

My favourite example of irreversible change is a fried egg!

And mine is a meringue!

IRREVERSIBLE CHANGES

An irreversible change is a change that takes place and *cannot be reversed to change the material back to its original state*. Imagine you are at a bonfire night party. You would be surrounded by all sorts of irreversible changes!

The wood on the bonfire is burning. As it burns, it changes from *wood* to *ash*. There is nothing you can do to reverse that change! As the fireworks are lit and they start to burn, they *cannot be changed back into their original state*.

Imagine you are cooking eggs. As you fry them in the pan, the whites change *from a clear, runny material to an opaque, rubbery texture*. This is an irreversible change. No matter what, you could not change the eggs back to their original state.

Imagine you are having meringues for pudding. Once the meringue mixture changes in the heat of the oven, from *white fluffy foam to a hard crispy shell*, it can *never be changed back*. This is another example of an irreversible change.

QUICK TEST

Put 'R' for reversible or 'I' for irreversible next to each of these changes:

1. Chocolate melting in a pan ____
2. Butter going soft and runny at a picnic ____
3. Eggs being poached ____
4. Ice cubes melting ____
5. Coal burning ____

ANSWERS 1 = R   2 = R   3 = I   4 = R   5 = I

HAVE A GO ...

Can you think of any other foods that can be changed reversibly or irreversibly as they are cooked? Make a list.

ROCK SOLID!

ROCK TYPES

Rocks can be found everywhere! When you go to the beach, you can see cliffs: these are made of rock. Pebbles on the beach are rocks – and even sand is sometimes made from tiny ground up pieces of rock. (Sand can also be partly made up of ground up shells)

Rock is used for many things.

- houses
- castles
- bridges
- churches
- walls
- pavements and floors
- roofs
- monuments and memorials

Rocks can be classified according to how HARD they are.

Rocks such as granite are hard. Granite is used to build things because it is hard and strong.

Chalk is not very hard. It crumbles easily. It would not therefore be a good material for building houses, as the walls would crumble!

THE USES OF ROCKS AND SOILS

Rocks and soil are used for many purposes. Houses are built, for example, from *stone*, *bricks*, and *slate*. However, did you know that glass is also a product of rock? It is produced using sand – and sand is rock that has been worn down into tiny particles.

TYPES OF SOIL

When you think of soil, you probably get a picture in your mind of a dark brown, crumbly substance. However, there are many different types of soil in different places. The colour and properties of the soil depend largely upon the base rock that the soil is made from.

Sandy soil – has a pale colour and water drains through easily.

Clay soil – sticky, orange or blue clay does not drain easily and puddles lay for some time after rain. It dries out with huge cracks on the surface.

Chalky soil – pale colour, drains quickly. It is a thin, poor soil that not many plants are able to grow on.

Peat – this dark, crumbly soil is made from ancient, decayed, plant material rather than rock particles. It holds lots of water.

So the soil on my football boots might contain clay?

Which might explain why you stay stuck to the spot and never get the ball!

★ top tip ★

What type of soil is there in your area? Can you find out what type of rock the base rock is?

QUICK TEST

1. Name three types of soil.

2. Name three types of rock.

3. Which is harder – chalk or granite?

HAVE A GO ...

Can you can talk about different types of soil and their properties?

ANSWERS 1 any sensible answer including: sandy, clay, peat, chalky
2 any sensible answer including chalk, granite, marble, limestone, sandstone
3 granite

55

SOME LIKE IT HOT!

CONDUCTING HEAT

Some materials <u>conduct</u> heat very well.

Think of a metal spoon that has been left in a steaming cup of coffee – it gets very hot indeed! Metal is a material that conducts heat well.

That is why saucepans are made from metal; they heat up quickly. However, the handles are usually made from another material, such as plastic or wood, because they are poor conductors. This means that you are less likely to burn your hands!

Now I know why Grandad always talks about wearing his thermals in cold weather!

Mum said it's the layer of trapped air that keeps him warm, YUK!

THERMAL INSULATORS

Thermal insulators are materials that keep things warm. Your duvet, fleece coat or woolly socks are good examples of insulators. Insulators help to prevent heat being lost. Funnily enough, it is the air in many of these things that makes them good insulators! The inside of a duvet, for example, is filled with feathers or fleecy wadding. These both trap large quantities of air. Cork flooring is also a good insulator for the same reason; it contains a high proportion of trapped air. Wearing layers of clothing, rather than one heavy topcoat, keeps you warmer for the same reason – the trapped air. Air is a poor conductor of heat, so the heat is less likely to be lost.

Creatures living in cold climates often have downy layers of fluffy fur or feathers next to their skin to act as insulators to keep them warm.

★ top tip ★

You could use a 'forehead' strip thermometer, or a stick thermometer if you have one, to measure the temperature of the water in each cup. If not, see which feels the hottest to the touch.

QUICK TEST

1. What is a thermal insulator?

2. Name two materials that are good thermal insulators.

3. What is a thermal conductor?

4. Name two materials that are good thermal conductors.

ANSWERS 1. Something that helps prevent heat loss. **2.** Feathers, fleece. **3.** Something that conducts heat very well. **4.** Metals, liquids.

HAVE A GO ...

Remembering to ALWAYS be careful with hot liquids, put some warm tap water into four plastic cups. Leave one as it is and wrap the others in different materials, such as paper, bubble wrap, cotton wool, fabric. After ten minutes, see which is warmest.

IT'S A MIX-UP!

BE A RESEARCH SCIENTIST!

You are going to carry out an experiment and record your findings just like a professional scientist. You will need:

* An empty two-litre plastic fizzy drink bottle

* Scissors

* Plain white kitchen paper towels

* Water

* Old container and spoon for mixing

* Sand or fine gravel; if not available use coffee grounds (not instant coffee granules)

WHAT TO DO

1. Carefully cut off the top third of the bottle. Take off the cap and throw it away.

2. Turn the top of the bottle upside down and push it into the other part of the bottle, like in the picture on the right.

3. Press the kitchen towel into the bottle.

4. Mix the sand/grit/coffee with the water.

5. Pour the mixture through the apparatus you have made.

6. What happened? Where is the water? Where is the solid?

7. Write a report, with a diagram, of what you did and the things you found out.

I've always seen myself as a great scientist!

A mad scientist, maybe!

HAVE A GO ...

What other mixtures can you separate using a filter? What different materials are filters made from?

59

TEST ROUND-UP

SECTION 1

1. Name a material that fits each description:

Pliable _____

Opaque _____

Transparent _____

Brittle _____

2. Mark these materials as thermal conductors (T) or thermal insulators (I):

Metal _____   Polystyrene _____

Cork _____   Air _____

Wood _____

SECTION 2

1. How are rocks used in everyday life?

_____

2. Name three types of rock _____

_____

_____

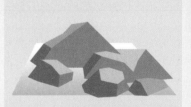

SECTION 3

1 What process would you use to separate an insoluble solid from a liquid?

_____

2 What process would you use to separate a soluble solid from a liquid?

_____

SECTION 4

1. How would you explain what is meant by the words:

   Solid
   _____
   _____

   Liquid
   _____
   _____

   Gas
   _____
   _____

2. Can you name an example of each?

   _____
   _____
   _____

3. Fill in the missing words using the box below:

   When water is _____ it starts to change from a liquid to a

   _____. The water has become _____. If the water

   vapour hits a cold surface, it changes _____ again, from a gas

   to a _____. This is called _____.

   | vapour | heated | condensation | liquid | gas | state |

I thought that was a bit hard.

Now, talking of materials, do you mean as hard as stone, or as hard as polystyrene – make it clear!

61

GRAVITY

The Earth *pulls things down towards itself* **with a force called** <u>gravity</u>**. The Earth is very large, and has a great mass, so the pull of the Earth's gravity is very strong.** *It is gravity that makes things fall when they are dropped.*

Other planets make gravity too, as does the moon. Have you ever seen film of astronauts on the moon? They bounce about, because *the moon has a weaker gravitational pull than the Earth.* **This is because the moon is smaller than the Earth.**

In deep space, there is no gravity. Scientists call this <u>zero gravity</u>.

So, if there were no gravity, things would float away when I dropped them? Excellent! I want to live in deep space!

FRICTION

Have you ever tried to slide on an icy playground? Did you get far? Do you think you would have managed to slide very far if there had been no ice?

Friction is created when *things are pulled past each other*. The *rougher the surface*, the *greater the friction* created. The *smoother the surface*, the *less friction* is created.

Friction helps us to *grip the ground* with our shoes as we walk. The tread on the soles of your shoes makes them rough and *creates friction*, even on quite smooth floors.

FEEL THE FORCE!

★ **top tip** ★

Try sliding on different surfaces, but be very careful. Can you predict which ones will let you slide the furthest?

QUICK TEST

1. If you dropped them at the same time, which of these would fall to the ground first?

   a. An orange

   b. A marble

Give a reason for your answer.

ANSWER Both would fall at the same rate, because gravity affects them equally.

HAVE A GO ...

Can you explain why things fall to the ground when we drop them?

63

IT'S ELECTRIC!

ELECTRICITY

We cannot see <u>electricity</u>, but we can see what it does. We use electricity in the home for light, heat and cooking. This electricity is called <u>mains electricity</u>. We also use electricity for toys and games, but this is a different, safer type that we get from a <u>battery</u>. This is the type of electricity we use for experiments in school and it is perfectly safe.

Electricity is not stored in a battery. Electricity is made or generated inside the battery when the chemicals inside react with one another. When a battery has gone flat, it just means that all the chemicals have already reacted with one another – they are all used up. Once there is no more reaction between them, there is no more power.

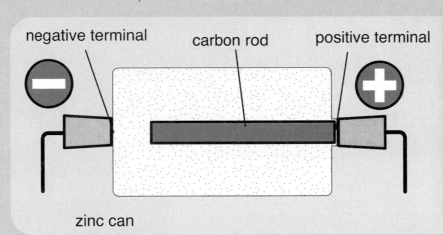

negative terminal   carbon rod   positive terminal

zinc can

Never try to open a battery, as the chemicals inside are strong acids and could hurt you.

CIRCUIT SYMBOLS

Symbols are used by scientists to represent pieces of equipment:

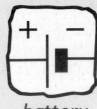      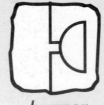   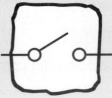

battery   *bulb*   *buzzer*   *switch*

ELECTRICAL CIRCUITS

Electricity flows through wires like water through a pipe. The *battery acts like a pump*, pushing the current through the wire. If a bulb is connected to a battery by wires in a circuit, the bulb or lamp will light. If the flow of electricity around the circuit is broken, the lamp will not light. A *switch* may be included in a circuit to *break the flow of electricity* and *turn the bulb on and off.*

Metals are good conductors of electricity, so wires are made of copper, a soft metal that can be stretched thin without breaking. The copper wire has a protective coat of plastic, which does not conduct electricity.

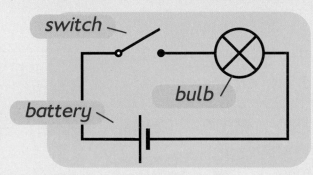
switch
bulb
battery

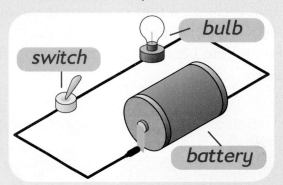
switch
bulb
battery

These questions suit my electric personality!

★top tip★

Mains electricity can be very dangerous and can kill you if you do not act sensibly. You should never plug things in or touch switches with wet hands, or you can get an electric shock. For the same reason, never poke anything into a plug socket.

QUICK TEST

1. What do the following circuit symbols stand for?

   a.    b.

2. What sort of materials are good conductors of electricity?

3. Name four things in your home that use electricity.

ANSWERS **1a.** Bulb **1b.** Battery **2.** Metals

HAVE A GO ...

Can you explain to someone what is inside a battery? Remember, never try to open one!

SOUND

Sound is a <u>vibration</u> in the air. Imagine you can hear a guitar being played. The sound you hear is made when the strings vibrate, which causes the air around them to vibrate. The <u>vibrations</u> in the air enter your ear, and your eardrum vibrates. This, in turn, makes the tiny bones inside your ear vibrate. A message is sent through a part of your ear, called the <u>cochlea</u>, through a nerve to your brain, telling you that you can hear guitar music.

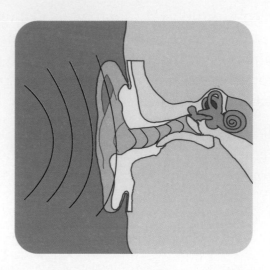

SOUNDS GOOD!

SOUND TRAVELS IN WAVES

Sound travels through the air in waves. These waves are invisible, but we can see how they might look with a special instrument called an <u>oscilloscope</u>. This measures the <u>amplitude</u> of the sound. That just means how much energy a sound has or how loud it is.

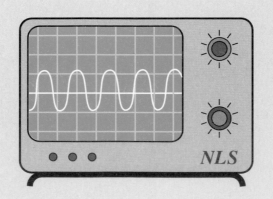

NLS

★ **top tip** ★

Never put or poke anything in your ear, because the eardrum is very delicate and thin, so is easily damaged. If this happens, you will be unable to hear properly.

HOW IS SOUND MEASURED?

Sound is measured in <u>decibels (dB)</u>. Very loud sounds can damage your ears. That is why you see people wearing ear mufflers when they are using noisy tools, like pneumatic drills. They *muffle the sound* and help to prevent damage. Ears can also be damaged by *infections and illnesses*, although most of these can be treated by the doctor. *Wax blocking your ears* also affects your hearing, and because the mechanics of the ear age, some people become *hard of hearing* when they get old.

Sounds good to me!

Sounds lovely and peaceful to me!

QUICK TEST

1. What unit do we use to measure sound?

2. What does amplitude mean?

3. How can hearing be damaged?

HAVE A GO ...

Can you explain to someone how we hear sounds?

ANSWERS **1.** Decibels (dB) **2.** How much energy a sound has. **3.** Very loud sounds, ear infections and illnesses.

DAY, NIGHT AND SEASONS

Did you know that the reason why we have day and night and the four seasons, is because of the movement of the Earth as it spins in space?

The Earth <u>orbits</u> around the sun once every 365 and a quarter days. This is what we call a year. The moon takes 28 days to orbit the earth. The seasons are caused by the Earth tilting over as it turns. When the north of the Earth is tilted towards the sun, our days in Britain are longer and warmer. This is spring and summer. When the north of the Earth is tilted away from the sun, we have shorter, colder days – autumn and winter.

THE EARTH – AND BEYOND!

THE SUN

It looks to us as though the sun moves across the sky during the day. *The sun does not move; it is the Earth that moves.* As the sun rises, we see it in the east. At midday, the sun is at its highest in the sky. This makes shadows look very short as the sun is shining directly overhead. The sun then seems to 'set' or 'go down' in the west.

sunrise *midday* *sunset*

★top tip★

Measure shadows at different points in the day – early morning, lunchtime and in the evening. Mark the outline of the shadow you have chosen on the floor with chalk and then compare them. You can see how the Earth rotates.

QUICK TEST

1. What causes the seasons?

2. During which part of the day is the sun at its highest in the sky?

3. Is it the sun or the Earth that moves during the day?

HAVE A GO ...

Can you tell someone why the sun seems to rise in the east and set in the west?

ANSWERS 1. The Earth tilting over as it turns. **2.** Midday. **3.** The Earth.

69

ATTRACTION AND REPULSION

Have you ever heard the phrase, 'opposites attract'? In the case of magnets, that's absolutely true! Magnets have a north pole and a south pole. If you put the north pole of one magnet next to the south pole of another magnet, the magnets will be attracted to each other and will pull together. If you put two south or north poles together, they will repel and try to push away from each other.

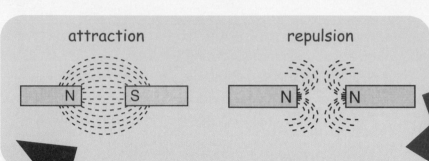

attraction   repulsion

N   S   N   N

★ top tip ★

Learn the sentence 'Opposite poles attract, like poles repel.' Learning science facts is a bit like learning spellings or tables in maths.

MAGNET MAYHEM!

ATTRACTIVE MATERIALS

What materials do magnets attract?

Magnets attract metals containing iron, such as steel. They also attract cobalt and nickel. Have you ever played a game using magnets? There is a game where a magnet on a string attached to a pole is used to catch 'fish' with metal tips. The game uses magnets and the attraction of metal to magnets. You can make your own game using pictures you have drawn and cut out, with metal paper clips attached. Make a pole with a pencil, string and a magnet.

MAGNETS WORK THROUGH MATERIALS

Magnets can work through other materials, depending on the strength of the magnet and the thickness of the material.

A magnet can attract an object through paper or card, for example. You can test this by placing paper clips on paper or card and moving them around invisibly with a magnet underneath.

Using magnets to attract through other materials can be fun. For example, you could make a spooky haunted house scene where ghosts, furniture – whatever you like – move invisibly … with a little help from your magnet!

QUICK TEST

1. Which of these materials will be attracted to a magnet?

   iron filings   plastic pen lid   leaf   paper clip
   pebble   chalk   drawing pin   jelly sweet
   sewing needle

2. Fill in the missing words from the box below:

   Magnets have a _____ pole and a _____ pole. When two south poles or two north poles are held near each other they will _____. This is because two like magnets will always _____ one another. When a north and south pole are held near each other, they will _____ because opposites always _____.

   south   north   attract   repel
   attract   repel

Opposites attract? That must be why I like Sam, then ...

Yuk!!

HAVE A GO ...

Make sure you know which combination of poles on magnets attracts and which repels one another.

ANSWERS   1. Iron filings, paper clip, drawing pin, sewing needle.
2. North, south, repel, repel, attract, attract.

71

TRICKS OF THE LIGHT!

SOURCES OF LIGHT

We see things because light is given off from an object or <u>reflected</u> by it. However, people are sometimes confused about whether a thing is a light source or is just reflecting the light.

The sun is a source of light, because it makes light; it is a burning ball of fire. The moon is more confusing because we talk about the moon 'shining' – but in fact, all the moon does is reflect light – the light given off by the sun.

 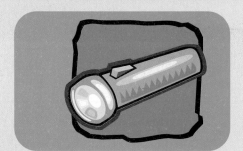

A lamp is a <u>source of light</u> and so is a torch. They actually make light.

A fire is a source of light, for the same reason, and so is a candle.

Other things seem to shine so brightly that it would be easy to get confused. A mirror, glass, glittery surfaces, metals and tin foil all shine – but they are not sources of light. They are just very good reflectors. This is because they have very smooth, shiny surfaces.

DOES LIGHT BEND?

Light travels in straight lines. We can see evidence of this when we look at a shadow. Since light cannot bend around objects, the light blocked by an object shows up as a shadow. We see light travelling in straight lines clearly at night when we use a torch, or the headlights on a car, or see the beam of light that shines out of a lighthouse.

When light hits an object, it bounces off and enters our eyes. This is how we see things.

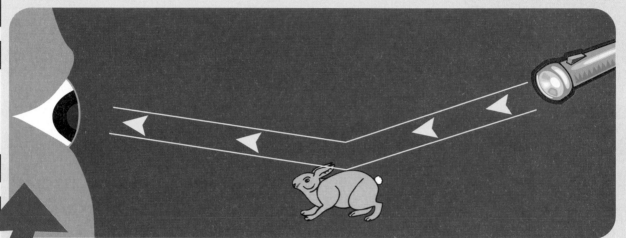

★top tip★

If you can't decide whether an object is a light source or a reflector, try to imagine what it would do if you shut it in a dark box. Would it glow? Then it's a source of light!

I need some new reflectors on my bike to help me be seen at night.

The way you ride, I'd buy some floodlights!

QUICK TEST

Which of these things are sources of light?

sun   moon   water   mirror   headlight
television screen   tin foil   copper pan

ANSWERS   Sun, headlight, television screen.

HAVE A GO ...

Can you explain to someone how light bounces off things and helps us to see?

MAKE A SINGING BALLOON!

WHAT YOU NEED

- **Big round balloon**

- **Small coin**

WHAT TO DO

1. Stretch the neck of the balloon and poke the coin inside.

2. Blow up the balloon – be CAREFUL! You don't want to get the coin in your mouth!

3. Tie the balloon neck to trap the air and the coin inside.

4. Hold the balloon between your hands and move it in circles. You need to make the coin start to roll on its edge around the inside of the balloon.

5. Put your ear on the balloon and listen. What can you hear?

6. Does the sound change at all as the coin slows down and falls over?

WHAT IS HAPPENING?

When the coin moves fast, it causes the balloon to vibrate quickly. Objects vibrating quickly make a high-pitched sound. As the coin slows down, the pitch of the sound gets lower. Clever, isn't it?

Can you invent another investigation to explore how sound works?

Well, Mel proves this theory right! She charges about quickly and makes high-pitched noises ...!

HAVE A GO ...

Would using a bigger or smaller coin in this experiment change anything? Have a try!

TEST ROUND-UP

SECTION 1

Draw a circuit diagram that contains:

A bulb   A switch   2 batteries

SECTION 2

1. How does friction help us to stay upright on an icy morning?

_____

_____

2. What force stops us from floating off into space? _____

3. What unit is used to measure sound? _____

4. What would happen if you put the north poles of two magnets near each other?

_____

_____

5. What would happen if you put the south poles of two magnets near each other?

_____

_____

6. What would happen if you put the north and south poles of two magnets together?

_____

_____

SECTION 3

Ring the pictures below that show a source of light.

SECTION 4

1. What do scientists mean when they talk about there being 'zero gravity' in space? What are the effects of zero gravity?

    _____

    _____

2. How do we hear things? _____

3. Can light travel around objects? _____

4. How are shadows made? _____

5. Are these substances solid (S), liquid (L) or gas (G)?

    water _____   milk _____

    steam _____   oxygen _____

    ice _____   carbon dioxide _____

    cheese _____   chalk _____

I'm off to test the action of gravity on an object repeatedly launched into the air!

What he means is he's going to jump up and down on his bed ...

NATIONAL TESTS

ABOUT THE NATIONAL TESTS IN SCIENCE

The National Tests in Science take place alongside the tests for English and Maths in May of each year. The tests are designed to show how much you have learned during your time at primary school – not just how much you have learned in Year Six!

You will be tested on many different topics, covering all areas of the National Curriculum for science. That means you will find questions on life and the living processes of plants, animals and humans; materials such as rocks and soils; and physical processes such as electricity, forces and magnetism.

Questions will also test your ability to read data such as graphs and your knowledge of investigations and how to set up experiments. These topics are all covered in this book.

Your teachers will also assess your work, and the results of these assessments, and your tests will be reported to your parents in July.

Although your results are used in League Tables, these tables are just to show how well your primary school is doing, compared to other schools. The results of your tests are not considered when a secondary school offers you a place, but they may use the results to help to put you in your first teaching groups in the core subjects of Science, Maths and English.

LEVELS OF ACHIEVEMENT

The National Curriculum divides up work into eight levels. By Year Six, you are expected to reach about Level 4. The General Science papers themselves will test all abilities from Level 3 to Level 5. The papers A and B each carry the same amount of marks and last 35 minutes

PREPARING FOR THE TESTS

The most important thing you can do is KEEP CALM! These tests are important, but don't get worried about them. You can only do your best and if you have listened in class and worked your way through this book, you will be very well prepared indeed!

Make sure you have lots of rest and spend time relaxing with your friends just before the tests. There is no point cramming the night before, but a quick read over the notes you have made, together with this book, will help to reassure you that you are prepared.

Remember – important though they are, the results of your KS2 Tests will soon be in the past as you start your exciting new career at secondary school!

1. PLANTS

a. What are the names of the parts of the plant?

1. _____

2. _____

3. _____

4. _____

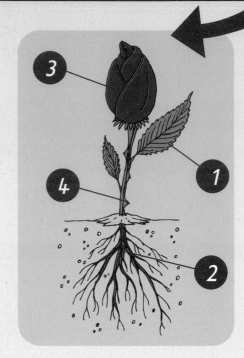

b. What is the function or job of each part?
   Join the correct label to each name:

leaf   root   stem   petals

| to attract pollinating insects with smell and colour | to hold the flower up in the air for pollination and to carry water to all parts of the plant | to anchor the plant in the soil and draw up water and nutrients | where the plant makes food using light from the sun |

c. What do most plants need to grow? Circle the correct answers:

water   wind   salt   light   beetles   nutrients

the correct temperature   a cool temperature

d. How are seeds dispersed or spread?
   Name four ways:

   _____   _____

   _____   _____

2. HABITATS

a. Look at the habitats and animals in the pictures below. Match the animal to the correct habitat and describe two ways in which each animal has adapted.

b. Draw arrows to show the direction in which energy flows along this food chain.

c. Which living thing in the food chain is the producer?

_____

d. Which is the primary consumer?

_____

e. Which is the top carnivore?

_____

3. MATERIALS

a. Look at the table below. It shows some of the materials you may find in your home, what they are used for and why those particular materials were chosen: their properties. Unfortunately, the table has got mixed up. Can you use a line to join each material with what it has been used for and why it was chosen? The first one has been done for you.

material	use	properties
stone	window	conducts heat well
wood	window frames	transparent – you can see through it
plastic	cushion covers	easy to clean; hygienic
fabric	saucepans	soft and warm to touch
glass	walls	strong and secure
metal	food storage boxes	strong, but light and easy to cut to size

b. Which of these materials are natural and which are synthetic (made by people)?

Chalk _____

Plastic _____

Leather _____

Polystyrene _____

Wood _____

c. Give reasons for your answers.

_____

_____

_____

_____

_____

4. LIFE PROCESSES

a. There are seven life processes that all living things share, but what does each word mean?

Match the words to the correct meaning:

Nutrition	Get rid of waste
Locomotion	Produce young
Sensitivity	Feed
Respiration	Move
Excretion	Breathe
Maturation	Feel things
Reproduction	Grow and change

b. Which of these things are alive? Draw a circle around them.

ladybird

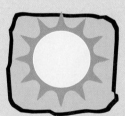
cat

sun

tree

rock

mirror

glass

83

5. PHYSICAL PROCESSES

a. Which of these circuits will light the bulb? Tick the complete circuits.

1.
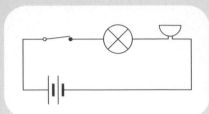

2.
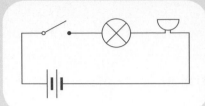

3.
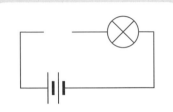

4.
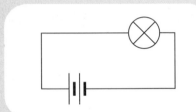

5.

6.

b. Which of the following things are powered by electricity?

toy soldier

teddy

light bulb

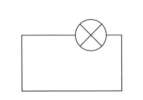

games console

remote control car

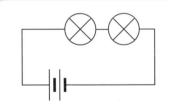

book

NATIONAL TEST PRACTICE ANSWERS

1. Plants   **page 80**

a. 1. Leaf 2. Root 3. Petals 4. Stem

b. Petal – to attract pollinating insects with smell and colour
Stem – to hold the flower up in the air for pollination and to carry water to all parts of the plant
Root – to anchor the plant in the soil and draw up water and nutrients
Leaf – where the 'food' is made using light from the sun.

c. Water, light, nutrients, the correct temperature

d. Wind, animals, birds, water, explosions

2. Habitats   **page 81**

a. Desert – camel – humps to store water, leathery eyelids and long silky eyelashes to keep out sand, splayed feet for walking on sand.

Seashore – anemone – retractable tentacles for sifting water for food means the creature can take shelter from the drying sun and wind when it is exposed by the tide. Its rubbery foot helps it grip the stones and not be washed away by the waves.

Tropical forest – spider monkey – toes for gripping and agile fingers for gathering food. Tail long and flexible for gripping trees.

Arctic – penguin – downy underfeathers to keep it warm, waterproof outer feathers to keep it dry. Streamlined shape for swimming.

b. Draw arrows to show the direction in which energy flows along this food chain.

Sun → pondweed → tadpole → heron

c. Producer = pondweed

d. Primary consumer = tadpole

e. Top carnivore = heron

3. Materials   page 82

a. Stone – walls – strong and secure
   Wood – window frames – strong but light and easy to cut to size
   Plastic – food storage boxes – easy to clean; hygienic
   Fabric – cushion covers – soft and warm to the touch
   Glass – window – transparent – you can see through it
   Metal – saucepans – conducts heat well

b. Chalk – natural
   Plastic – synthetic
   Leather – natural
   Polystyrene – synthetic
   Wood – natural

c. Chalk is a stone, leather is animal skin and wood is from trees.

4. Life processes   page 83

a. Nutrition – feed
   Locomotion – move
   Sensitivity – feel things
   Respiration – breathe
   Excretion – get rid of waste
   Maturation – grow and change
   Reproduction – produce young

b. Which of these things are alive? Draw a circle around them.

   Ladybird, cat, tree

5. Physical processes   page 84

a. ✔ Circuit 1 – cell, bulb, buzzer and closed switch
   ✔ Circuit 5 – cell, bulb
   ✔ Circuit 6 – cell, two bulbs

b. Light bulb, games console, remote control car

TEST ROUND-UP ANSWERS

Test round-up – Plants   **pages 12–13**

Section 1

1. Petal   **2.** Stem   **3.** Leaf   **4.** Stigma   **5.** Anther   **6.** Stamen   **7.** Root

Section 2

Join each part of the plant to the correct description with a line.

Plant grown in bright sunlight, plenty of water

Plant grown in the dark, plenty of water

Plant grown in bright sunlight, not enough water

Section 3

Ring round these:

1.   Moisture   air   correct temperature

2.   Insects   wind

3.   Wind   water   birds   animals   explosions

Test round-up – Animals   **pages 30–31**

Section 1

1.   A habitat is the place where organisms such as plants and animals live – the seashore, woods and rainforests are examples.

2.   A community is the collection of plants and animals that live in a particular habitat.

3.   An ecosystem is the name given to a community and its environment.

Section 2

1.   Seaweed = primary producer
Periwinkle = primary consumer
Crab = secondary consumer
Otter = top carnivore

2.   Metamorphosis = great change.

Section 3

✔ Thick waterproof fur
✔ Wide tail like a paddle
✔ Large front teeth for gnawing wood

Stage 1   Stage 2   Stage 3   Stage 4

Section 4

Use the **Venn diagram** below to sort these animals into groups:

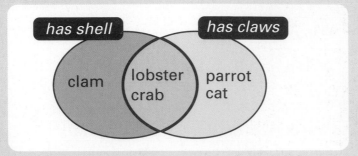

has shell has claws

clam lobster crab parrot cat

Section 5

Match the microorganism to the correct result:

fungus = mouldy bread

bacteria = gastroenteritis

virus = 'flu

Test round-up – Human life pages 42–43

Section 1

1. Fats, carbohydrates, protein, plus fibre, water, vitamins and minerals

2. Circle

   (apple)/apple pie   (carrot)/carrot cake

   (strawberries)/strawberry jam   (oranges)/orange squash

   Because they are all fresh and unprocessed – full of vitamins and minerals

3. To help us to digest our food

4. Draw a healthy dinner with food chosen from the basket below:

   Any combination that only includes small quantities of sweets, crisps and fizzy drinks.

Section 2

1. For grinding tough plants

2. For killing prey and tearing meat

3. Circle

   (incisor) indicator   omnivores (molar) mole molecular

   (canine) ceramic capillaries

4. Support, movement, protection

5. Red cells, white cells, plasma, platelets

6. Fill in the missing words:
   Red cells carry oxygen around the body.
   White blood cells attack microbes and fight disease.

Test round-up – Materials   **pages 60–61**

Section 1

1. Name a material that fits each description:
   Any suitable materials including:
   Pliable – rubber
   Opaque – wood
   Transparent – glass
   Brittle – plastic

2. Metal – T
   Polystyrene – I
   Cork – I
   Air – I
   Wood – I

Section 2

1. building walls, roofs, houses, paving, churches etc.

2. Any sensible answer including chalk, granite, marble, limestone, sandstone

Section 3

1. Filtration

2. Evaporation

Section 4

1. **Solids** have a <u>definite shape</u>, are quite <u>heavy</u> for their size, and <u>do not flow</u>.
   Liquids take the <u>shape of the container they are in</u> and <u>flow easily</u>.
   Gases take the <u>shape of the container</u> they are held in and <u>flow easily</u>.

2. **Solid** example: stone   **Liquid** example: water
   Gas example: air

3. Fill in the missing words using the box below:
   When water is <u>heated</u> it starts to change from a liquid to a gas. The water has become <u>vapour</u>. If the water vapour hits a cold surface, it changes <u>state</u> again, from a gas to a liquid. This is called <u>condensation</u>.

Section 1

– Any circuit diagram that contains a bulb, a switch and two batteries.

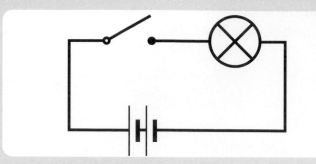

Section 2

1. Friction helps our feet to grip the ground so we don't slip.

2. Gravity

3. Decibels (dB)

4. Repel

5. Repel

6. Attract

Section 3

Standard lamp, street light, headlight.

Section 4

1. Zero gravity means that there is no gravitational pull, so things float off into space.

2. Sounds are vibrations in the air. The vibrations cause our eardrum to vibrate. The small bones in our ear move and our nerves send a message to our brain telling it we have heard a sound.

3. No – it travels in straight lines.

4. Shadows are made when objects block the light. Light cannot bend, so the shadow shows up where the light has been blocked.

5. Water – L   Steam – G   Ice – S   Cheese – S   Milk – L   Oxygen – G
   Carbon dioxide – G   Chalk – S

GLOSSARY

Adapt, adaptation, adapted The way in which plants and animals change over time to cope with the conditions in their environment.

Amplitude How loud a sound is. A loud sound such as a shout has a high amplitude, and a quiet sound such as a whisper has a low amplitude.

Anther The anther is the 'bobble' that carries pollen inside a flower. It is a male part of a flower.

Artery An artery is a blood vessel that carries blood away from the heart.

Bacteria Bacteria are tiny microorganisms. They can cause an illness such as gastroenteritis or they can be helpful. It is bacteria that turn milk into yogurt.

Battery A source of energy, created by a chemical reaction.

Biceps The large bulgy muscle on the upper side of your upper arm.

Brittle Brittle materials are stiff and break easily. Glass is brittle.

Camouflage Things or animals that are camouflaged are disguised to match their environment. A leopard's spots hide the animal in the dappled light of the jungle.

Canine teeth Canine teeth are the sharp pointy teeth used for tearing food.

Carbohydrate Carbohydrate is a food group that includes foods such as pasta and cereals.

Carnivore, carnivorous Carnivores are animals that eat meat – other animals.

Cells Cells are the building blocks that make up all living things – plants and animals. They are very tiny.

Characteristics Characteristics are features such as colour and size. Every plant and animal – including humans – has characteristics. Some are inherited from our parents, while others are created by the environment in which we live.

Chlorophyll A green chemical found in plants that helps them to make food using the energy in sunlight.

Circulatory system The system of blood vessels such as arteries and veins that carries blood around the body.

Classification The process used by scientists to sort things into sets.

Classification key A key used to sort plants and creatures into groups.

Climate The usual weather in a particular place.

Cochlea The shell-shaped part inside the ear that helps us to hear sounds.

Community The creatures and plants that live together in a particular habitat.

Condensation When steam hits a cold surface it changes state from a gas to a liquid and turns back into water. The water is called condensation.

Conduct, conductor An electrical conductor is a material that allows electricity to pass through it, and a thermal conductor is a material that allows heat to pass through it.

dB The symbol that stands for the unit that measures sound – decibels.

Decibels The unit that sound is measured in.

Diagram A scientific drawing is called a diagram.

Digestive system The system made up of internal organs such as the stomach and intestines that is used to break down food inside the body.

Ecology Ecology is the study of living things in their surroundings.

Ecosystem An ecosystem is a community of plants and animals and its environment.

Electricity A source of energy transported by wires and stored in batteries.

Energy Energy is used whenever work is done. Food gives you chemical energy, for example. Other forms of energy include sound, heat, light and electrical energy.

Environment An environment is the natural surroundings of an animal or plant.

Evaporation When a liquid changes state into a gas, the process is called evaporation.

Fair test A fair test is a test where everything is judged to be equal at the start of an experiment – except the particular thing being tested for. For example, if you were testing for the effects of light on plant growth, it would not be a fair test if one plant was bigger than the other at the beginning of the experiment.

Fats Fats are a food group. Butter and nuts are fats.

Fertilisation When the male and female cells join together to make a new life, the process is called fertilisation. This happens with plants and animals.

Fibre Fibre is found in foods such as cereal, fruit and vegetables. It is bulky and indigestible in itself, but helps us to digest other foods.

Filtration A process used to separate soluble and insoluble materials, e.g. sand and water.

Food chain A food chain shows the way in which energy is passed from the sun to plants and is then eaten by animals, who are in turn eaten by other animals.

<u>Food web</u> Food webs are similar to food chains but show much more complicated feeding relationships.

<u>Friction</u> The rubbing together of moving objects that slows them down.

<u>Fungus</u>, <u>fungi</u> A fungus is a plant that does not make energy using sunlight. It absorbs goodness made when other plants and animals decay.

<u>Germinate</u>/<u>germination</u> When a seed starts to grow, the process is called germination.

<u>Gravity</u> Gravity is the force that makes objects fall to the ground when you drop them. Everything in the universe is attracted to everything else by gravity.

<u>Habitat</u> The place where plants and animals live is called a habitat. Examples include the seashore and woodland.

<u>Herbivore</u>/<u>herbivorous</u> An animal that is totally vegetarian – eats only plants – is called a herbivore. An example would be a cow.

<u>Hinge joint</u> A joint of the body that works like a door hinge, e.g. knee or elbow.

<u>Igneous rock</u> Igneous rock is made when molten lava from a volcano cools. An example would be granite.

<u>Incisor</u> Our front teeth, which we use for biting into our food, are called incisors. Rabbits have large incisors for cropping grass.

<u>Insoluble</u> Materials that will not dissolve are called insoluble. Sand, for example, is insoluble in water.

<u>Internal organs</u> The organs inside our body such as our heart and kidneys are our internal organs.

<u>Irreversible change</u> A change that cannot be reversed, such as an egg being fried or wood being burned.

<u>Leaf</u> A leaf is the food factory where a plant uses sunlight to make energy.

<u>Life cycle</u> A life cycle describes the changes and growth an organism goes through from birth to adulthood.

<u>Light energy</u> Light energy is given off by anything luminous such as street lights, candles and fires.

<u>Mains electricity</u> The electricity that we use in the home when we plug something into a wall socket.

<u>Mass</u> Mass is the amount of matter that something contains. We buy potatoes according to the mass of potatoes in the bag. Weight is the force created when gravity pulls on an object. How heavy an object is depends on its mass.

Metamorphic rock Metamorphic rock is made when rock is changed over time by extreme pressure. Examples include slate and marble.

Metamorphosis Metamorphosis is when a creature undergoes a complete physical change when growing from child to adult, e.g. a caterpillar becoming a butterfly.

Microorganism Tiny organisms such as bacteria and viruses.

Mnemonic A mnemonic is a silly sentence made up to jog your memory. The sentence 'Richard Of York Gave Battle In Vain' is used to remind people of the order of colours in a rainbow – Red, Orange, Yellow, Green, Blue, Indigo, Violet.

Molars The back teeth used for grinding food.

National Tests See SATs.

Nutrients The goodness in food eaten (or in the case of plants, in the soil) is known as nutrients. This would include vitamins and minerals.

Opaque Things that do not let light through – and we cannot see through – are opaque. This would include black sugar paper, for example.

Orbit An orbit is the journey made by a planet or asteroid around another planet or star.

Organism A living thing.

Oscilloscope A piece of equipment used to measure sound waves.

Ovary An ovary holds eggs – female cells – in animals and plants.

Ovules An ovule is a female cell – an egg.

Petal A petal is the part of a plant that is brightly coloured and sometimes scented to attract insects to plants.

Photosynthesis This is the name of the process used by plants to change light energy into food.

Plaque Sticky material that causes tooth decay if it is not cleaned away. It is formed by bacteria acting on food fragments.

Plasma The clear fluid full of salts that makes up a large part of the blood.

Platelets The tiny pieces of blood cell that help to make blood clot.

Pliable Pliable materials are bendy and do not snap easily.

Pollinated, pollinating, pollination This is the name of the process carried out by insects or the wind as pollen is carried from one plant to another.

Predators Animals which hunt and eat other animals are called predators.

Primary consumer The name given to herbivores in a food chain – animals that eat plants, the primary producers.

Primary producer Plants are producers in the food chain. They use the energy from the sun to make or produce food.

Properties of materials Properties of materials are features such as hard/soft/heavy/strong.

Protein Protein is found in foods such as cheese and beans. The body needs this food group for growth and repair.

Pulse Your pulse is the beating you feel in your wrist or neck that shows how your blood is flowing around your body. After you have exercised, your pulse rate is quicker than normal, as your heart is beating faster.

Red cells Cells found in the blood that carry dissolved oxygen around the body.

Reflect, reflected, reflection When light or heat bounces back off a surface, we say that it has been reflected.

Reversible change A change that can be reversed, such as melting ice being frozen again.

Root The part of a plant that anchors it in the soil.

SATs Standard Assessment Tests (also known as National Tests). In the primary school, SATs are carried out at the end of Key Stage One (at age 7) and at the end of Key Stage Two (at age 11). Tests are taken in English, Maths and Science.

Secondary consumer In a food chain, a secondary consumer is an animal that eats primary consumers. In the food chain lettuce – slug – hedgehog, the hedgehog is the secondary consumer.

Sedimentary rock Sedimentary rock is formed when sediment such as mud falls to the bottom of a sea or lake. Examples include sandstone. Fossils are found in sedimentary rock.

Seed dispersal Dispersal means the way in which things are spread out or scattered. Seeds are dispersed by the wind, animals, water, explosions and birds.

Shadow Shadows are made when light is blocked by an opaque object. Shadows are the absence of light.

Soluble Something that dissolves. Salt and sugar are soluble in water.

Source of light Something that gives off light and does not merely reflect it, e.g. the sun.

Species A species is a group of similar animals which can breed with one another, such as different types or breeds of cat.

<u>Stamens</u> Stamens (male) are the tiny sticks that hold the anthers up in the air inside a plant. They do this to make sure wind or insects carry the pollen to another plant.

<u>State</u>, <u>states of matter</u> Solid, liquid and gas are states of matter. When we say a substance has changed state, we mean it has changed, for example, from a solid to a liquid – as when ice melts and changes into water.

<u>Stem (plant)</u> The stalk of a flower that holds the flower up, so it can be pollinated by insects or the wind. The stem acts as a pipe, carrying water and nutrients to all parts of the plant.

<u>Stigma</u> The stigma (female) is the sticky part at the centre of a flower that catches pollen.

<u>Tertiary consumer</u> The tertiary consumer is the top carnivore in a food chain. It is not eaten by anything else in the chain. In the chain seaweed – scallop – penguin – walrus – orca whale, the tertiary consumer is the orca whale.

<u>Thermal conductor</u> A thermal conductor is a material that allows heat to pass through easily. Metal is a good thermal conductor. That is why cooking pans are often made from metal.

<u>Thermal insulator</u> A thermal insulator is a material that does not allow heat to pass through it easily. Wood is a thermal insulator. That is why the handles on cooking pans are often made from wood.

<u>Transparent</u> A transparent material allows light to pass through it. We can see through transparent materials such as glass easily.

<u>Triceps</u> The triceps is the muscle on the underside of your upper arm.

<u>Veins</u> Veins are the blood vessels that carry blood back to your heart.

<u>Venn diagram</u> A diagram made from two circles to show how items may be grouped or classified according to characteristics they share.

<u>Vibration</u> A quick shaking backwards and forwards movement is called a vibration. Sounds cause the air to vibrate, for example.

<u>Virus</u> A virus is a microorganism that causes illnesses such as 'flu and the common cold.

<u>Water vapour</u> Another name for steam. A vapour is a type of gas.

<u>White cells</u> Found in blood, white cells are the defence system of the body. They fight bacteria and viruses.

<u>Zero gravity</u> The scientific term for there being no gravity in deep space.